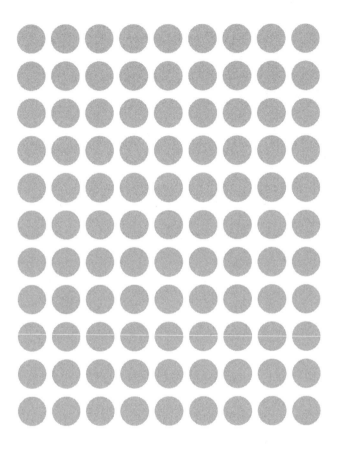

GOAT IN THE SNOW

EMILY PETTIT

BIRDS, LLC | AUSTIN, MINNEAPOLIS, NEW YORK, RALEIGH

Birds, LLC
Austin, Minneapolis, New York, Raleigh
www.birdsllc.com

Cover designed by Joshua Elliott
Interior designed by Michael Newton

Library of Congress Cataloging-in-Publication Data:
Pettit, Emily
Goat in the Snow/Emily Pettit
Library of Congress Control Number: 2011938984

First Edition, 2012.
ISBN-13: 9780982617762
Printed in the USA

GOAT IN THE SNOW

FOR RITA THE MAGNIFICENT

GOAT IN THE SNOW

●

● ●

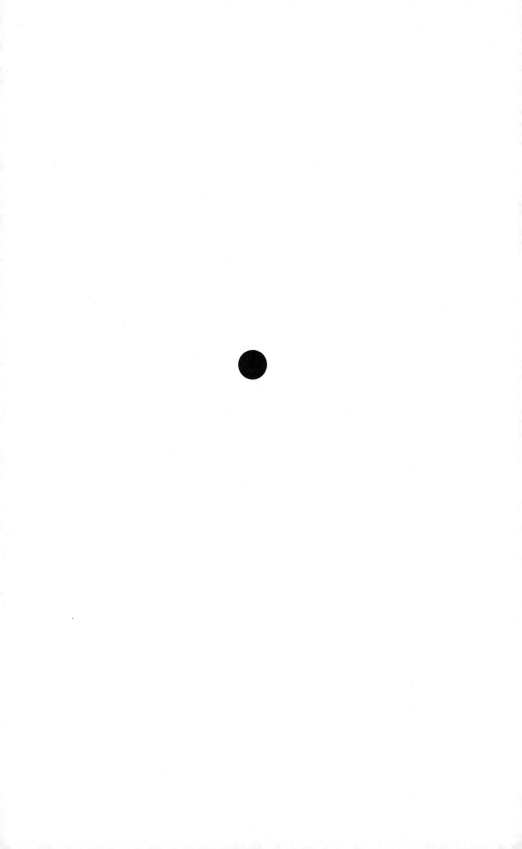

RED WINGS COLLAPSING

What do you call a field of black telephones ringing?
A problem? Sometimes I make ridiculous gestures
with my arms and legs, and call it dancing. So you see
it is not the color of your hats that has guided me here.
If I give you a red bird it means more than if I give
you a story about a blue hat. When I am not a nuance
expressed in echoes, I am quite modest and quite murky.
Once in modest and murky water, I had a very disturbing
conversation with a boat. This boat said, *I don't want to know*
that much about every goddamn whale. This boat blew me away,
as the unexpected often does. I want to know more about normal
accidents, owls misplaced in the arctic, breathing in code,
dead fish on the sidewalk, extinction in the meadow, red wings
collapsing. I don't want to know what to call a field of black
telephones ringing. Have you ever built a giant mess with tiny tools?
You are not alone when you make ridiculous gestures
with your arms and legs, and call it dancing. We all are.

HOW TO BE RESPONSIBLE

When the respiratory system says,
I don't feel like being a network right now,
you have developed a giant disorder.
You breathe out of order. It doesn't totally suck.
It staggers. It's not like being a hook.
It's more like being a hook ladder.
Like the silence that sometimes accompanies the
unexpected. What are your ears hearing?
I mean move over falling days,
I am attempting to be responsible.
No imitation breathing. It is inadequate.
What to do with what you have heard?
Hammer, anvil, stirrup—the bones
that form a bridge in the ear need to
form a bridge elsewhere in the dark.
Darkness a bet you make again
and again. You are asked to accept
the fantastic. It's so fantastic.
Accept it. Someone says, *Emotions*
don't have brains. And someone is right.
It's a different way to dance. Mind
no longer content to move around
the circumference, mind makes a big leap,
becomes a telescope ladder. A significant
vertical exposure. An altered heart.
I forget approximately.

HOW TO RECOGNIZE WHEN YOU HAVE
BEHAVED BADLY AND BEHAVE BETTER

I put my hand on your hand. Mostly I meant to
be good. It was the shaking sky and what I wanted
to see below. It is always shaking where I am.
What do you know from the shoulder up?
I know you can only watch the plane
until you can't. Prominent cloud features are not far
from my mind. It's an attempt to protect
both of our mind circumferences from being mistaken
for a shark that stops swimming. And other forms
of disaster. I apologize. I would do anything
for a different look from you. Animals in the ocean
make mistakes too, maybe. And our memories.
I know memory is remarkable and unpredictable.
And I am meaning to be better with what I know.
I know now is not the time to take up flying.
You say, *I'm watching you*. And I say, *No, I'm watching you*.
I am the government on the moon and
I mean to let you forgive me.

GOAT IN THE SNOW

A goat is not a sheep, though I know people
who have made this mistake not meaning
to be flippant. This is not how to start a fire

with sticks.
I do not believe that music comes from a place of silence,
just as life does not begin from a point of stillness.

After passing the farm with the goat
it was important to slow down.
Hello goat. Hello officer. So easy to lose track

when going downhill. It isn't always easy to become calm
after such an outburst of excitement.
Some people don't have their animals down.

I myself would not recognize a mongoose,
but I know the word *mongoose* and I know it refers
to an animal, a mammal. I imagine it to be

long-torsoed and beady-eyed, but I don't know.
Remember when we were at that place
where the floor tilted? That was a place

where we could close our eyes.
They were closed. They were open.
We were accumulating information.

Sometimes this meant we were filing things
and we hate filing things and so it goes.
Later we were laughing.

If you fumble, you'd better laugh.
I've seen a goat chase a llama and it's hard
to take that seriously. Some things

we will repeat over and over again.
I said, *I want to be a fly on the wall.*
Someone said, *Be a goat in the snow.*

We like to think of shipwrecks
as beautiful fuck-ups
and that goats' eyes are the secret to goats.

I think if I had a soul it would be saying *soul.*
To move quietly past a fence without hesitation
is what a goat does.

HOW TO HIDE FROM ANOTHER

Identification kept in a lockbox. Identification
kept in a lost place. What surrounds that thing
that should be left alone? And what surrounds you?
Rain. You say you want some new weather.
You say you cannot help yourself. Swan in a sad swamp.
You are such an ambulance stuck in traffic.
Rope encased in plastic. I wear no identification.
I would prefer that I am not described or located.
You say you need a bridge. I say we'll get you a bridge.
What is the word for an order that makes sense?
You say you are traveling from place to place,
hoping to find a temporary delay. A departure
from reasoning. If you need a canyon, here's a canyon.
Sometimes you leave something so that someone can find it
later. I know you don't want an umbrella, but here's an
umbrella. And here's another umbrella. And another.
Another. Another.

HOW TO RECOGNIZE A STRANGER

Shame had got us down. A monsoon
impulse. A ship on fire flying through the sky.
We are like, *We need a banquet and a meeting.*
It's not a new idea. It's as old as a tiger
angrily lashing its tail. Improving, oh how
difficult it can be! Like glowing in the dark.
Like twice the inventions in half the time.
We stay awake. We stay awake. A horse
running in small circles. This is brain injury
awareness. We cover our faces with our hands
to communicate our displeasure at being so
confused. We put all of our octopi in one eye.
It's not pretty. It's nothing to scream about.
We scream and scream. Stay so silent,
give up all your small machines and still
you might be standing still. Someone says,
Don't put all of your octopi in one eye. Problem solved.
We would like to speak to the operator.
Are we speaking to the operator?
The problem is solved. We etch-a-sketch
the problem being solved. It's pretty
complicated looking. It looks like a duck,
until we shake it. And when we shake it,
it looks like a new stranger, a fancy glance,
too many telephone poles, a twitching mind.
We are working on recognizing the noise a twitching
mind makes. That we would know this noise,
that we would act accordingly.

HOW TO STOP LAUGHING WHEN YOU LAUGH
AT INAPPROPRIATE TIMES

While you explained how to survive
a long fall, I could not stop thinking about
how to escape from a sinking car.

There is a one-armed man staring
at me or the photograph above
my head. Split apart with a gap,
that mouth a gape.

My brain from a bleeding height
is not so pretty a picture.

I've been trying to devise a plot,
plan or scheme, an illicit or illegal one,
one that is ill advised in some way.
Extortion isn't always effective.

When I blow everything up
I promise I won't put everything back
together in the old and comfortable ways.

Try to maneuver like a spacecraft
passing sufficiently close to a planet

in order to make some relatively detailed observations
without landing.

Real children notice arches.
Fake children do not.

THINGS HAPPEN IN THE NIGHT
AND THEN IT IS NOT NIGHT

How it is flickering. How there are deer
and cattle too. How horns might mean
something. How to become star-shaped.
How some people can sing. How you
hold a hammer and practice and skill,
it's all related to the bones in the body.
You are my giraffe in this igloo, in this
orange. And the table is orange too.
And the orange is on the edge. And I am
on the edge. And later I will repeat, *I am
on the edge.* The edge is both the point
at which something is likely to begin
and end. This is the astonishing power
of generosity! How it is infinitely complex.
How it cools outside. How we wonder
is this acceptable? How you hear so often,
Ok ok ok ok ok. I'm ok.

HOW TO FIND A ROBBER

Don't look. Don't look anywhere.
I am behaving like such an animal.
I found a field full of crows.
I am selling people bad transit tickets.
I am sure of it. Row boat row boat.
Brain chemicals boat style rocking.
There's your voice. There are some
well given instructions. When it comes to
performing some of the most difficult
and laborious operations of abstract thought,
I fail. *Hey person, I love you!* I kick at rocks.
I pretend to be a very treacherous fox.
Foxes will also eat vegetables
when they are available. Are you available?
I am learning this skull. Ants all over
this small broken blue egg.
Because I might be in a boat.
Because it made me feel different.
Because I don't want to be a fool.
Hey someone, I want to want less.
I stand in corners. I am not corrected.

IN THE INSIDE OUTSIDE

Everyone was the best at the party.
This is what I like to say sometimes. Despite
everything. Regardless of all circumstances.
There are feelings and feelings. Someone
is bad to someone else. Someone is bad to you.
You are bad to someone else. Little fish look
to the side. Owl eyes saw a dagger. Time
is tricky and everywhere in different places
all at once. Electricity is the only way to explain it.
Yet like controlled movement, I don't understand
electricity. A vocabulary of alarm stuck in my mouth.
Like a giraffe inside a giraffe, inside a giraffe,
inside of a lion. An arsenal of weather. How is it
going to change you? To let go of something
you've never held. Someone says, *Get get vulgar.*
It is like that. That, that feels familiar in a false way.
Some would say it is what's going on in the front
of your brain that makes you a person. So I say,
What's going on in the back? And someone says,
Your eyes.

HOW TO BE ALONE IN A SHAPE

I do what I was going to do anyways.
I do it all day. A neat and foreign spider.
I don't have any trees though. I don't
have any trees though. There's this idea
about feeling good every day. Someone says,
You've got to be pleased and satisfied.
Some birds have rhythm. Someone found
a 35,000 year old flute. Music I cannot make.
Drugs I cannot make. When fear is not a set
shape, I do what I was going to do.
I do it all day. There are efforts though,
to stop the errors of thinking and doing.
Hidden in the angles are ideas I have
about gravity following different rules.
I think, *What are the action opportunities?*
Like get dedicated. Here is an inventory
of operating systems. Insight. Insects.
Assembling all pieces of anything you can
find. And it is easy to say things. It is harder
to mean things. Build a pyramid. Have no
idea why.

YOUR JOB IS TO LOOK BOTH WAYS

It is not your birthday but I am giving
you this candy bar and science. A flashlight
in your mouth. You build a map in layers.
Tiger stripes on the brain. It's ten seconds
until seven and if you lead me by the hand
I will leave. What do you believe might happen?
Once I drove a money truck and nothing happened.
Keep your eyes out. Keep keep your symmetry
breaking bubbles. Whack that tiny piece of space.
It has to do with the world and how it came to be.
And when a particular dangerous animal enters
the scene, how urgently everyone shouts.
Yell *Lion!* Yell and yell. We can hear this ant cry.
Did you ever? It's like our deal with gravity,
it continually deceives. You might not know it
but that's a dome and that's a dome. Can you produce
a sun dog? Here's an eye. Here's some light.
Here's 22°. Look over there. I want you to
measure that with your fence. Daylight played a role
in establishing its form. I'm not a scientist of the device
designed for light travel, but I've seen the
evolution of a shadow. It is not your birthday
but I see you. You are a detective. You are a detective
and you are hiding.

HOW TO APPEAR NORMAL IN FRONT
OF YOUR ENEMY OR COMPETITOR

Damn icebox and my fist, I didn't hit it.
The prison lights twitch in the distance
and we aren't right dreaming about stuffed
lamb's heart. Picture going to the butcher shop
and asking for the ingredients. I can't,
it makes me laugh. You may not believe
your invisibility an advantage, though it is.
The better beekeeper knows to be still.
A dead bird's wing frozen to the trunk of a car.
No one wants to remove it. I know
about the impenetrable system of communication
and I say let's destroy it. *Tell us how,* they say.
Not now, I say, *doubt me later.*

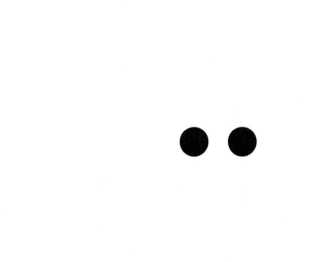

(RADIO SILENCE)

I looked you in the face. Up on a wire it's hard
to be anything other than awkward. An old hat
sitting in an airport smoking lounge. Mechanical
children singing in unison. Anyone speaking
in unison. Being bad with a machete. A tailor
with no hands. A manmade lake in the middle
of a concrete landscape. Hanging on to
a fire extinguisher. The noise a mouth makes
when it opens to speak. A little foot in a big shoe.
In a footrace you are a faster runner and I am an arrow
not moving, just hanging out in one of those slings
people keep arrows in. Completely out of place.
You are familiar with the rules, are you not?
When I bring you to beautiful places you must
forgive me for bringing you to beautiful places.
I looked you especially in the right eye and I didn't
say a word.

BUILDING SMOKE DETECTORS

The world's worst wind chime won't stop
striking our ears. Hazard and bizarre.
Did we look to the wrong part of the floor?
Did the floor fall flat? We don't want to get mysterious
about numbers. We can't wrap our minds around
a black hole. Maybe the floor isn't the problem.
Maybe the blinking could be better described.
What are we going to do with the big City
and the Bible? Big blinking City. Big blinking Bible.
Your lighter is too big for you. It takes up your whole
hand. Be careful. The wooden sign says, *Frost.*
The billboard says, *Casino.* Someone says, *Hazard
and bizarre!* We call this laboratory confusion.
The world is potentially over and we are interested
in potential. Now go back to where you were
and try not to light everything on fire.

EVACUATION PROCEDURES ARE NEVER CLEAR ENOUGH

Walking towards the lit capital dome
the cross-street we cross reads, *Dodge Street,*
so we dodge. We do not qualify for The Rock, Paper,
Scissors World Competition. Our system of logic
does not apply appropriately. Our mountains
and moon are upside down. Our peacocks
and elephants are upside down. There is a metal chip
in the dog's back. There is no dog here.
And yes, we think the building looks like a road.
And no, we haven't collapsed, but we need beams.
Our fingers would be on fire if someone hadn't broken
them off. Someone says, *Science is happening.*
The sky, never close-mouthed, though generally quiet,
says, *I am much more complicated. I am not blue.*
This is interactive sound information meeting
with a smart crash. The red water here is not red,
the green wind is not green, the orange house is not orange,
and the blue roof like the sky is not blue. We are
much too big for this room we are not in.

HOW TO THROW THINGS AROUND

Moon hanging from a crane. Four ducks
in a row, one without a head. Jello
and fake limbs produced on the same belt.
Flammable and inflammable mean the same thing.
The line between paranoia and reasonable
concern is not always clear. Stopping banana boats
looking for nuclear weapons. Tricky bananas,
radioactive bananas. What do we know
about potassium? We know more about bats.
Some bats can fit through dime-size holes.
Some bats can carry the smallest bombs.
If the bats don't bother you, you can visit us.
And kangaroos, kangaroos can't bother you either
if you'd like to come over. There is a kangaroo
loose in our house and we're in the water,
short an oar. No we don't give a toss.
We are busy scattering. We scatter the water
and the light scatters itself.

HUGE GENTLENESS

Someone says, *Look above or below!*
It's a planet being mercilessly pummeled
by small burning objects. Accurate blows
to our best parts. What shall we call these
places? Our best parts. It's a fence
dispute. The noise the neighbors make.
Like several rulers gaining prominence
all at once. Like legs lingering by
one another. Like when you touch history
that's not your own. *That, that,*
that, that's what a fish might think.
For a fish, a fin might be its best part.
You happen naturally. A transmission
of sound. An airplane noise
in the sky. Instability in the atmosphere
that disrupts the flow of wind.
Oh if we could learn through osmosis!
How the intervening air can make
a mountain appear more or less blue.
I watched you in the snow, on the steps,
out the window, in the water.
I feel like the most distant point,
the final part of a finger. Good response,
but no fire. There was no fire, but a
good response. Our effective understanding,
a movable barrier. Our feelings like fish
on fire far away, but not that far away.

HOW TO START A FIRE WITHOUT STICKS

Get up. Get up and pretend your head isn't full
of tiny broken sticks. It will be worth it to walk
through the door such a complicated mess,
crazy to such purpose. One way to torture a person
who is sleep deprived is to pretend the house is on
fire. Look very serious and say, *Fire! Fire! Fire!*
Look very serious and say, *Water! Water! Water!*
Look very serious and say, *You built a better body*
of water. Yes you did. Where did you find such a
stunning embankment? Pretend you put out the fire
with the better body of water. Pretend you are
a medium to large marine mammal. I will be
a fly on the wall dressed as a person, a person who
has complicated ideas about what constitutes a wall.
No doubt I'm a little faded, dejected, incognito,
noncommittal. I only do practical things.

HOW TO FIND WATER SOMEWHERE ELSE

Bridges are often the place where you see
other bridges. This is what a brain scan
can look like. It's a make-believe pizza place.
It's funny and it hurts. The ignition forgets
we are breathing with our ears. It's a bond.
And we're just getting started. Singing songs
makes your brain grow. Ordinary intention
is not enough. Someone says, *Ordinary*
intention is not enough. You design a rocket ship.
I abandon a fingerprint file. You design a rocket
ship. You design another rocket ship.
Real town, fake blizzard. Is this what loving
someone is like? This looking at someone doing
something and doing something. And it keeps
going and going and it keeps on going.
It is a new kind of emergency. Very much falling.
Calling attention to a shy fact. Very confusing.
In need of microscopic analysis. It's all danger danger
danger by the river.   But in the house.

HOW TO FIND WATER IN THE ORANGE

Someone explains how to cook something.
Someone else does not listen. In the lake
look at how the fish are not cooking
anything. At the bottom and in other
places there is no cooking. It takes geography.
It eliminates it. When I am having toast
I keep not having toast. What would be
a liberation? A blue screw in the cement wall.
Orange. I've got my telephone. My telephone
does telephone calls. I was waiting again.
My heart beats fast fast fast. Is your heart
beating fast? A pattern of frequent worry.
Pick up geography. Wanting a new big easier.
Take me out. When the glass shatters,
it shatters too far. I have will. Where has it gone.
How you might want to show what you know.
Sometimes you go out there. At least as far as
your window can see. Or rather, no farther than
a window your window can see. Why not
want your own window? Want water. Want
water where you are. You want to get struck
with a change. I go I go I go. But come back
come back come back.

HOW TO HIDE A FIRE

When everything fell down, the big
eyes didn't see it. No one did. You see,
my people are always falling down.
These are today's headlines!
Lungs are neato and very lobular.
The curtain is blowing though
the window is closed. People are
doing magic and blushing. It's a bad day
for chickens. Disco is dead.
And this is why one shouldn't talk shit.
There is always more news. People
knowing each others' whereabouts
on a need to know basis. Something
in front of you reflecting that behind you.
People jumping up and down. People
thinking it feels good. Yesterday I was
a misguided fire truck. Today, again I am
a misguided fire truck. I know that
when the smoke attaches itself to the air,
our eyes also get attached there. There
is forever a sound I am trying
to identify that hides in this commotion.
A rooster roams around this place,
a sitting duck.

HOW TO PUT AN UNCONSCIOUS
PERSON INTO A RECOVERY POSITION

I like to talk on the phone in the governor's suite.
I like to say, *Let's say they can have balloons.*
Let's say it's a pleasant feeling in the face.
I want you to understand my intentions.
Don't you   you relax. An element in the
air. It looks like the sky is on my hand.
Even when intentions are not enough,
there they are, intentions! An elephant
not sleeping. How you hold a hammer.
Understanding conduct like understanding
a complex and lively bee. Experiments in terror
suggest seeking solace in an abandonment
of consistency. Specific and purposeful action
is often taken to conceal this fact. A satellite
shot down resulting in the shutdown
of all sky communication. It takes new
shapes. All of this technology and nothing.
A fox face. It takes focus on the fingertips.
Your hand. Your hand, with which you influence
your surroundings. It's there for grasping.
It's there for knowledge, detailed or not.
Welcome back to where you are. Everyone leaves
work. No one says anything. Where are you?
I am here, with you.

HOW TO SHOOT A SLINGSHOT

At first the coyotes are mistaken for sirens,
a grave mistake that begins in our feet.
Sometimes you go forward and sometimes you go
backward and sometimes you just stomp out fires.
Another picture you drew of the list of things
you have to do. The speed of train travel changing.
The spiders paranoid. All of the typewriter repairmen
incarcerated. Everyone distracted by the need
to bite one's own leg. And we, we are still leaning
with great energy, still interested in sideways glances.
Here are as many questions as blinks. As blanks.
Here might enter some controversy. Damn feet.
Damn disagreement. If this is breaking your heart
close your eyes. If we swept you away forgive us.
We'd like to depart without warning.

HOW TO HOLD A TINY EYE

Sometimes things get really beautiful really fast.
Good evening to you! Let's get nice right now.
I know you know I have a tiny eye, so perhaps
I'm not to be trusted. It is an unpredictable eye.
My tiny eye says, *You bet*. My tiny eye likes to look
at sure shadows. Likes the precipitation
accumulating on the ladder. Likes to lock itself
to sad machines. My tiny eye forgets far
into the distance. My tiny eye might take you
on a carefully-coordinated-for-you voyage or
my tiny eye might take you on a walk into the deepest
dark and leave you there. The edge is often an eye's
route to understanding and this I am trying to understand.
And yes it's true I keep my tiny eye hidden.
My tiny eye is out of control. My tiny eye wants
to have its own ideas and it does. For a fire
my tiny eye would do almost anything.
For a feather where wouldn't my tiny eye fall?

GO AIRPLANE, SWAY TREE

This time there is an entire dead bird
body to remove. Give me your documents,
I want to know a whole lot of things
about things I know nothing about.
Somewhere there are monkeys
who speak with their hands. Mostly
they discuss food. Sometimes birds.
The monkeys say (sign), *The swans
displease us.* A love affair ending poorly
between a submarine and a satellite
displeases me. That the monkeys may fight
shouldn't displease anyone. Shouldn't surprise
anyone. Who needs a map of the friction
when the lightning looks like a plan?
Who needs to know why the airplanes go
or the trees sway? I want to know why
the weather changed when the door killed
the cricket. I want to know why it's peeping
that floods the air when we are waiting.
I want to know why I'm not whispering this
in your ear. Why it is that you can't hear me.

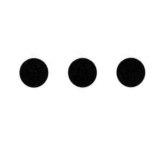

HOW TO HIDE AN ELEPHANT

All over town footprints are flying. When walking
on tiptoes we ignite suspicious minds. Hovering,
hanging out nowhere near the ground.
I'm on my way to the end of the world again.
Thirteen red barns in a row. A story on the news.
A mouse has died in the wall. I have a box
full of porcupine quills. I have a box full of
tiny tools. A box full of bees. Becoming information
is not necessarily a choice. A chance meeting
is not necessarily enough to change things.
If your reflection went missing what would you do?
Feel like a spider who has forgotten how to weave
a web. Try to remember where you last leaned,
where you last left no trace. Here is a tiny elephant.
Put it in your pocket and it can be the elephant in the room
that no one ever talks about.

HOW TO FIND LOST OBJECTS

This is no articulation of ethics.
I'm talking about hats,
and maybe goats.
Steel, a stem,
eyebrows, ivory.
I'm talking about peeling
an avocado.

I think chalk is chalk.

This is an opportunity.
Don't have an epiphany.

Chalk is a moose.

A spoon is a baby.
A creek is a shoe.
A satellite is a banjo.
Eternity is a branch.
A barn is yellow.
A puddle, a curtain.

I like my caverns dark.
Caverns should be.

Things here are uncomfortable
and that's a good thing.

There are willows
and windows,
twine and bones,
pillars and mercury,
bedrock and buffalo,
organs and apes,
tile and wax.

There is history by the meter.

I don't mean to chivvy,
nonsense, plain talk,
flapsauce, score,
rubbish, right,
scrawl, tuck,
hogwash, inside track,
drivel, proper,
prattle you.

The fish in the water
is right there.

No, there.

HOW TO BE IRRESPONSIBLE

You've forgotten where you put your map
of the basement. Remember the basement?
It's under the house. If you still had a shadow
it'd be dancing on top of the basement.
Too bad you lost the house. Now it will be
harder to find a door. Too bad you couldn't stop
looking out the window. An old problem.
Your shadow was the shape of you, you
thought you knew. I am obsessed
with an old problem and I have a brand new
megaphone. It is not a good thing. It is a most
significant and ongoing mistake. Do you
understand? This is not a normal interaction
station. Everyone is eating ice cream cones
in the rain. Everyone is grabbing at feathers,
looking stunning and rather serious. It's a puzzle
generator. It is the reflection of a disappearing
act. You should've known better than to
let the lions out. I let the lions out too,
but I'm not the zookeeper.

HAUL AND PULL

Things here are galling. We are tumbling over and between
the ice cap and the timberline. Who said you were brave?
And what do they know? You can wake up to more than one step
down or to urgent elevation. It looks like a scale drawing
of any side of a building. A call for immediate attention.
For now I think you'd better haul and pull.
Sitting next to a chemist, I need a cryptographer.
I'm not allowed to talk about it. Like the part of a parallelogram
that is left when a smaller similar parallelogram has been taken
from its corner. People are flocking to these small green areas.
Later we'll try to remove them, the tangles.
Later we'll try to provide access to something
previously unavailable. There are a couple of places
in which human activity is generally missing.
It's hard to fit in a hummingbird's bill. Clouds refuse to carry us.
There are quiet parts of our brains. We are not devout logicians.
We are logicians nevertheless. Strangely we ignore the detailed
part of the document that is printed in small characters.
We stand holding a suspended pivoting pole with a bucket
on one end and a counterweight on the other.
We do not cover our faces to become linked or united.
We thought we were constrained to obey certain masters.
This declaration was a lie. Reverse the circle. Boil it. Stir it.
Make it too good to be true. Involuntary trembling may ensue and
on these occasions where do we run? We do run.

HOW TO CAREFULLY CONSIDER
INTERSTELLAR SPACE TRAVEL

Let's consider how strange planets can be.
Planets can be so strange. My planet is a bandit.
My planet was banished. Now it's plunder,
plunder, plunder. And your planet? What about it?
Is it strong? My planet is full of fireballs. Fireballs
don't typically make noise. Did you know that?
What does your planet do when it's alone?
My planet spends a great, great, deal of time being shy
alone. To be shy alone is to have an unusual fact.
It's a bible in the oven. An ancient baby
mammoth. A distance which no measure makes.
If we develop a sufficiently powerful spacecraft
for the purpose of exploring interstellar space
will our minds succeed in growing sufficiently
elastic to survive the travel? Let's
make some entirely reasonable predictions.
No we will not survive the travel. Yes we will
survive the travel. That's interstellar space.
That's some time. That's an anatomical feature
on a baby's skull. There is a chance that the elasticity
we want will be ours. All there is, is a chance.
And everyone knows chances are strange.
And sometimes chances are like planets
that get too close to their stars.

IF IT'S NOT ONE THING, IT MIGHT BE EVERYTHING

Hello my mess! You certainly are looking fine
today, like such an extraordinary giraffe.
Please excuse my less than extraordinary appearance.
Had I known I would be encountering you today
I would have put this engine I have in this bucket I have.
I would have flown right into that dump truck,
not even blindfolded. Knowing it was coming.
Dump truck, dump truck, dump truck.
I would have let the dawn leak a little more.
You may burst or collapse in disbelief
when I tell you this, but I've been worried
about you. You've become such a parrot,
such a smalltime hustler of a mess.
Can't we have more on our mind than one
shoe at a time? One shadow. One infinite think.
Sometimes you need to purposefully blink
and say, *That's small shoes. That's long walking.*
You are looking at me like you don't know
what I'm talking about. You are looking at me
like this is a case of mistaken identity.
Someone shouts, *Today, everyone looks familiar!*

HOW TO LOSE LOST OBJECTS

This is the memory of a house, so no one lives here.
Here we like our emergencies savvy, ravens
flying low, close to our witness. Try standing
and watching yourself disappear. A new way
to see things is kaleidoscope style. When you walk
past a certain kind of light, you can cast
six different shadows all shaped like you.
One wakes every fifteen minutes. One waits
for a specific series of noises. The walls here
hold wind, whether you believe it or not.
Hey house, how come you terrorize with anchorage?
We would like to disprove the watched-pot-never-boils
theory, though our waiting chore seems on the verge
of destruction. Any not staying lost with the lost
thing feels like a betrayal. House full of tumbleweed.
Mouth full of tumbleweed.

HOW TO CONTROL A BLACKOUT

In the tall grass with their heads down
they held the shape of sheep, but one
couldn't tell for sure. Oh the uncertainty!
Someone says, *Your blood should stay
in your veins.* A flow of information
to the hand. I say to someone,
I don't know what I want. What I mean
to say is, *This here is a fuse box.*
I mean to say, *I know nothing about fuses.*
Did I say fuses? I meant to say facts.
I need to get good at tracking. Track
my own thought back to a black horse.
It's hard to carry a horse on your back.
It is an eyeful. It's like permutation symmetry.
It is a matter of experimental fact.
It's like standing in a fire pit. You are
standing in a fire pit. What do you say?
Someone will ask, *How did you get here?*
They'll give you a tune up. They'll say,
Tone it down. You'll be a wolf in the water.
You'll be a wolf in the water.

HOW TO MAKE NO NOISE

I think a bad thought and I am left wondering
if hope should ever be saved and if one was to
save it, then would one need to hide it?
And where would one hide it, if one had to
do so? Say there are ten thousand dead crickets
to deal with, go far away or don't.
Who could have known you could have
done that sort of damage without making
any noise. Your eye thinks light only travels
in straight lines. Burst these reports.
Forgiveness exists in the face of what isn't fair.
Now if you please, use your eyelashes to run
a dotted line through the sky. Compromise
quietly and practice (radio silence) when anyone asks
about your involvement. The crickets were cheap.
They were silent. In what direction do you look
when someone says something true?
The recognition of a quality. For example, to be
known for a great roar. Rain that runs down
your face in a certain way. I can't walk home
without startling a rabbit and I slam the door
so quietly shut.

HOW TO AVOID CONFRONTING
MOST LARGE ANIMALS

Most large animals are very small
if seen from very far away. If seen
from far away large problems
look like red and blue blinking
clusters, clashing against the lit
and littered dark sky, countless eyes
in the dark, blinking along the yellow
dashes lining the road, traffic two miles
long, stopped for a giant stag
not soon enough. Not enough time.
Not enough space. It makes it hard
to think about inventing new instruments
and inventories. Wanting to disappear
is different from wanting to die.
I want us to be exposed to a very
pleasing and impressive risk.
You show your neck, you show
your neck. You are saying, *Look
at my neck.* Can you love me?
Replicate a vocal pattern. You know
you know you know. It's all uncertainty
and your neck. You walk slowly
in a calm voice.

HOW TO HIDE AND STAY HIDDEN

Again I hang nothing on the line.
More people are killed by elephants
than sharks. More people are killed
by sharks than airplanes. I hear
in my shoulder all of these voices,
Are you in the sky? Are you at the zoo?
These voices are crying up the wrong
telephone pole, are raining down
the wrong gutter. Eyes open.
Here's to hoping. Here's to looking.
When I close my eyes and I see cranes,
heavy metal birds. Heavy machinery
wonder is where my head is. Damn
addictions. Damn dependence with
damaging effects. We like to think
we're obsessed with quality. It's so good
it's a crime. I love elephants. I feel
differently about sharks at different times.
Always I love heavy machinery and birds.
I especially love heavy machinery resembling
birds. I know cranes kill people too.
Though the number is a secret,
like where I am.

HOW TO KNOW THE WORTH OF WHAT

One must be an eye moving rapidly. A dance hall.
An electric train. A clever collision. I am knee high
to a duck, so this is a full-fledged challenge.
I walked far in the snow. *Some more ghost bread please.*
Oh what a declaration! What a hat with no head!
What a rocket anchor with no rocket.
The choice to attend, again the wrong choice.
Someone says, *I can tell you what anything is worth.*
A working stove is worth breathing out of order.
An unattained ideal is worth a telescope ladder.
An ice-cream factory, 100 dishonest chickens.
A single spotlight, a most favorable council.
A strange detail, all your love. Brain imaging scans,
a wind-up beetle. A dinosaur is worth
the establishment of a pattern. The sound of shifting feet,
the sound of shifting eyes. A misguided request,
imitation forgetfulness. A weathervane,
being quiet for a while. A major event. The coincidence
of discovery initiating invention. And I say to someone,
Please let go. I am trying to pay attention.

HOW TO BUILD A FIRE IN THE SNOW

Something broke. I knelt down to pick up
the pieces. They fell between my fingers.
This may indicate a failure to provide

a proper or reasonable level of care.
I don't want to be a paper tiger.
Better to be a paper wasp. Something good

that happens unexpectedly. To glide
through the air without propulsion,
in the way that a bird does without flapping

its wings or an airplane with its engine off.
Everything is so tricky and I like that.
To be a hover disc or sand. One of the amazing

things about color, that's different from your ear,
is your eye only sees one color. The individual
frequencies are lost. It only seems like a

particular shade of blue. These are my boat
shoes. I don't go on boats. A volcano
that is not extinct and still erupts occasionally

relies on a point or place at a lower level,
one below a surface. The snow is withdrawn
on the window and I am grateful that someone

knew that I did not know what I asked
when I asked, *What does it mean to purchase*
a ticket to a place with red water?

It was like something that happened by chance.
To fix this any digits of the hand will do.
And so what if the lights here are always off?

It's night and the lights are off.
In the dark a feather caught my shoulder
and it did not immediately let go.

ACKNOWLEDGEMENTS

Many thanks to the editors of the following magazines where some of these poems first appeared: *Conduit*, *DIAGRAM*, *Everyday Genius*, *FORKLIFT, OHIO*, *Fou*, *Glitterpony*, *H_NGM_N*, *Invisible Ear*, *Jellyfish Magazine*, *Octopus*, *PFS Post*, *Sixth Finch*, *SKEIN*, *Strange Machine*, *SUPERMACHINE*, and *Wolf in a Field*.

Many thanks to Octopus Books for publishing a chapbook *HOW*, in which a number of these poems appear.

Many thanks to Matthea Harvey, Alex Phillips, Dean Young, and Matthew Zapruder.

Many thanks to John Ashbery, Michael Barron, Luke Bloomfield, Shannon Burns, Rob Casper, Francesca Chabrier, Heather Christle, Meghan Dewar, Ben Fama, Rachel B. Glaser, Pam Glaven, Kevin Gonzalez, Nat Herold, James Haug, Rory Jenson, Kaylin Jones, Alix Kennedy, David Kermani, Ben Kopel, Seth Landman, Claire Lawlor, Mark Leidner, Lizzie Lenson, Lisa Olstein, Nathaniel Otting, Caryl Pagel, Katie Perry, Guy Pettit, Michael Pettit, Heather Reddick, Maya Sharpe, Meredith Simpson, Jordan Stempleman, Bianca Stone, Michelle Taransky, James Tate, Jen Tyson, Liz Van Dyke, Betsy Wheeler, Mark Wootton, Dara Wier, Amy Wilson, and Alix Zacharias.

Many thanks to Joshua Elliott and Michael Newton.

Many thanks to Dan Boehl, Justin Marks, Matt Rasmussen, Sampson Starkweather, and Chris Tonelli.

Emily Pettit is the author of two chapbooks, *How* (Octopus Books), and *What Happened to Limbo* (Pilot Books). She is an editor for *notnostrums* and Factory Hollow Press, as well as the publisher of *jubilat*. She teaches at Flying Object.